Diary

Created by M&M Publications.
Printed by CreateSpace, An Amazon.com Company.

ISBN-13: 978-1522972419
ISBN-10: 1522972412

Owner:

Date: ______________________

Dear Diary,

Owner name: ______________ Signature

Date: ______________________________

Dear Diary,

Owner name: ____________________ Signature

Date: ______________________

Dear Diary,

Owner name: ______________ Signature

Date: ____________________

Dear Diary,

Owner name: ______________ Signature

Date: ____________________

Dear Diary,

Owner name: ____________ Signature

Date: ____________________

Dear Diary,

Owner name: ____________________ Signature

Date: ______________________

Dear Diary,

Owner name: ______________ Signature

Date: ____________________

Dear Diary,

Owner name: ____________________ Signature

Date: ______________________

Dear Diary,

Owner name: ____________________ Signature

Date: ____________________

Dear Diary,

Owner name: ________________ Signature

Date: ______________________

Dear Diary,

Owner name: ______________ Signature

Date: ______________________

Dear Diary,

Owner name: ____________________ Signature

Date: ______________________

Dear Diary,

Owner name: ____________________ Signature

Date: ______________________

Dear Diary,

Owner name: ________________ Signature

Date:

Dear Diary,

Owner name: Signature

Date: ______________________

Dear Diary,

Owner name: ______________ Signature

Date: ______________________

Dear Diary,

Owner name: ______________________ Signature

Date: ____________________

Dear Diary,

Owner name: ____________________ Signature

Date:

Dear Diary,

Owner name: Signature

Date: ____________________

Dear Diary,

Owner name: ____________ Signature

Date: ______________________

Dear Diary,

Owner name: ______________ Signature

Date: ______________________

Dear Diary,

Owner name: ______________ Signature

Date:

Dear Diary,

Owner name: Signature

Date: ______________________

Dear Diary,

Owner name: ______________ Signature

Date: ____________________

Dear Diary,

Owner name: ____________________ Signature

Date: ______________________

Dear Diary,

Owner name: ______________________ Signature

Date: ______________________

Dear Diary,

Owner name: ______________ Signature

Date: ______________________

Dear Diary,

Owner name: ______________________ Signature

Date: ______________________

Dear Diary,

Owner name: ______________ Signature

Date: ____________________

Dear Diary,

Owner name: ____________________ Signature

Date: ____________________

Dear Diary,

Owner name: ______________ Signature

Date: ______________________

Dear Diary,

Owner name: ____________________ Signature

Date: ______________________

Dear Diary,

Owner name: ____________________ Signature

Date: ______________________

Dear Diary,

Owner name: ______________________ Signature

Date: ______________________

Dear Diary,

Owner name: ______________________ Signature

Date: ______________________

Dear Diary,

Owner name: ______________________ Signature

Date: ____________________

Dear Diary,

Owner name: ____________________ Signature

Date: ______________________

Dear Diary,

Owner name: ________________ Signature

Date: ____________________

Dear Diary,

Owner name: ____________ Signature

Date: ______________________

Dear Diary,

Owner name: ____________________ Signature

Date: ______________________

Dear Diary,

Owner name: ____________ Signature

Date: ______________________

Dear Diary,

Owner name: ______________________ Signature

Date: ______________________

Dear Diary,

Owner name: ______________ Signature

Date: ______________________________

Dear Diary,

Owner name: ____________________ Signature

Date: ______________________

Dear Diary,

Owner name: ______________ Signature

Date: ____________________

Dear Diary,

Owner name: ____________________ Signature

Date: ______________________

Dear Diary,

Owner name: ________________ Signature

Date: ______________________

Dear Diary,

Owner name: ____________________ Signature

Date: ______________________

Dear Diary,

Owner name: ____________ Signature

Date: ______________________

Dear Diary,

Owner name: ______________ Signature

Date: ______________________

Dear Diary,

Owner name: ______________________ Signature

Date: ____________________

Dear Diary,

Owner name: ____________________ Signature

Date: ____________________

Dear Diary,

Owner name: ______________ Signature

Date: ______________________

Dear Diary,

Owner name: ____________________ Signature

Date: ______________________

Dear Diary,

Owner name: ______________ Signature

Date: ____________________

Dear Diary,

Owner name: ______________ Signature

Date: ______________________

Dear Diary,

Owner name: ______________ Signature

Date: ____________________

Dear Diary,

Owner name: ____________________ Signature

Date: ______________________

Dear Diary,

Owner name: ______________ Signature

Date: ______________________

Dear Diary,

Owner name: ______________ Signature

Date: ____________________

Dear Diary,

Owner name: ____________________ Signature

Date: ______________________

Dear Diary,

Owner name: ______________ Signature

Date: ____________________

Dear Diary,

Owner name: ____________________ Signature

Date: ______________________

Dear Diary,

Owner name: ______________________ Signature

Date: ______________________

Dear Diary,

Owner name: ______________ Signature

Date: ____________________

Dear Diary,

Owner name: ____________ Signature

Date: ____________________

Dear Diary,

Owner name: ____________________ Signature

Date: ______________________

Dear Diary,

Owner name: ______________ Signature

Date:

Dear Diary,

Owner name: Signature

Date: ______________________

Dear Diary,

Owner name: ______________ Signature

Date: ____________________

Dear Diary,

Owner name: ____________ Signature

Date: ______________________

Dear Diary,

Owner name: ____________________ Signature

Date: ____________________

Dear Diary,

Owner name: ____________________ Signature

Date: ______________________

Dear Diary,

Owner name: ____________________ Signature

Date: ______________________

Dear Diary,

Owner name: ________________ Signature

Date: ______________________

Dear Diary,

Owner name: ______________ Signature

Date: ______________________

Dear Diary,

Owner name: ______________ Signature

Date: ______________________

Dear Diary,

Owner name: ______________ Signature

Date: ______________________

Dear Diary,

Owner name: ________________ Signature

Date: ____________________

Dear Diary,

Owner name: ______________ Signature

Date: ______________________

Dear Diary,

Owner name: ______________ Signature

Date: ______________________________

Dear Diary,

Owner name: ____________________ Signature

Date: ____________________

Dear Diary,

Owner name: ______________ Signature

Date: ______________________

Dear Diary,

Owner name: ______________ Signature

Date: ____________________

Dear Diary,

Owner name: ____________ Signature

Date: ____________________

Dear Diary,

Owner name: ____________________ Signature

Date: ______________________

Dear Diary,

Owner name: ______________ Signature

Date: ____________________

Dear Diary,

Owner name: ____________________ Signature

Date: ______________________

Dear Diary,

Owner name: ______________ Signature

Date: ______________________

Dear Diary,

Owner name: ______________________ Signature

Date: ____________________

Dear Diary,

Owner name: ____________ Signature

Date: ______________________

Dear Diary,

Owner name: ____________ Signature

Date: ______________________

Dear Diary,

Owner name: ____________ Signature

Date: ______________________________

Dear Diary,

Owner name: ____________________ Signature

Date: ____________________________

Dear Diary,

Owner name: ______________________ Signature

Date: ______________________

Dear Diary,

Owner name: ____________________ Signature

Date: ______________________

Dear Diary,

Owner name: ______________ Signature

Date: ____________________

Dear Diary,

Owner name: ____________________ Signature

Date: ______________________

Dear Diary,

Owner name: ______________ Signature

Date: ______________________

Dear Diary,

Owner name: ____________________ Signature

Date: ______________________

Dear Diary,

Owner name: ______________________ Signature

www.ingramcontent.com/pod-product-compliance
Lightning Source LLC
Chambersburg PA
CBHW072102280526
45788CB00006B/2366
9781522972419